The Five Keys

12 Step Recovery Without A God

The Five Keys

12 Step Recovery Without A God

Archer Voxx

Maze Publishing

Copyright © 2013 by Maze Publishing

All rights reserved. No part of this book may be reproduced or transmitted in any form or by any means, graphic, electronic, or mechanical, including photocopying, recording, taping, or by any information storage retrieval system, without written permission of the author.

ISBN: 978-1483921129

Printed in the United States of America

Retail ordering:

www.amazon.com

Wholesale ordering and general information:

Email: info@mazepublishing.com

This book is dedicated to my wife for her understanding and patience.

"We cannot solve our problems with the same thinking we used when we created them."

Albert Einstein

About This Book

The 12-Step program of Alcoholics Anonymous has been used successfully for addiction recovery worldwide. However, many individuals have difficulty using the program because they are not comfortable with its religious sounding content. These people are looking for a recovery solution that has a solid technical foundation, not something faith-based or religious in nature.

The 12-Step program is much more than it appears on the surface. The program has a strong technical foundation and has been successful because it is grounded in over 200 years of experiments with addiction recovery that came before it in the United States. This includes work in medicine, psychology, psychiatry, and spirituality. The religious language comes from only one of the program's influences.

The Five Keys provides insight into five areas of the 12-Step program that make the faith-based content transparent and allows you to use the program without a God or Higher Power.

Contents

Topic	Pages
• <u>Introduction</u>	1
• <u>Foundation For The Five Keys</u>	
The Newcomer Experience	6
Practical Considerations	10
Early Debate Over Religion	12
• <u>The Five Keys</u>	
Background	15
1. An Objective View of AA	18
2. Major Program Influences	24
3. The Spiritual Transformation	30
4. Universal Spiritual Principles	38
5. Neutral 12 Steps	43
• <u>Making It Work For You</u>	50
• <u>Bibliography & About The Author</u>	57
• <u>Appendix</u>	I - VII

Introduction

The 12-Step program of Alcoholics Anonymous (AA) is one of the most successful programs in history for addressing addiction. It has been used as a solution for alcohol, narcotics, gambling, sex, and other personal challenges. The program is also used by family members and friends of addicts for assistance with codependent behaviors that they have in common with the addict (Al-Anon).

The 12-Step program has been successful because it focuses on improving a person's self-esteem and relationships, and addresses the issues that are at the source of virtually all addictions. It accomplishes this through a sequence of actions that involve honesty, personal discovery, sharing, restoring trust, and providing assistance to others who are trying to address their addiction.

The primary reference book for the 12-Step process is *Alcoholics Anonymous* (often referred to as "The Big Book" of AA). The Big Book is a valuable resource for the recovering addict because it provides insight into the medical, psychological, and spiritual issues associated with the disease of addiction and advances a program for recovery. It has proven to be transformational for individuals with an addiction, regardless of their religious, political, or social beliefs and affiliations.

Whether you have strong religious beliefs, or hold to an agnostic or atheist view, it is apparent when you read The Big Book that it is a doctrine with significant roots in traditional Judeo-Christian religion. This statement is not a value judgment, but simply a fact. To make The Big Book and its 12 Steps more appealing and accessible to a broader audience, the authors introduced the concepts of "God of Your Understanding" and "Higher Power" to allow for an alternative to the traditional Judeo-Christian God. Although the authors provided this flexibility, The Big Book and its 12 Steps remain rich in other Judeo-Christian content. The references to prayer, turning your will over to God or a Higher Power, and related terminology and activities are prominent.

An individual's response to The Big Book, and their ability to use the 12-Step recovery program, falls into one of three general profiles. The first consists of individuals who find the 12-Step program comfortable because they have a strong religious foundation, or they can make it work with the concepts of God of Your Understanding or Higher Power. They trust that the spiritual, philosophical, and technical principles underlying the program are solid and that it will lead them out of their addiction. Faith in their God and the observation that the 12-Step program has worked for others are all they require to get started.

The second profile includes people who have a history with traditional religion but have become disillusioned with their faith over time. As far as their addiction goes, no amount of prayer, confession, and reflection has provided relief. The individuals in this profile find the 12-Step program reasonably straightforward from the standpoint of the religious aspects, but they do not believe that any program grounded in religion will provide a way out of their addiction. As a result, these individuals would prefer an addiction recovery process that is outside of religion—something that has a technical or scientific basis.

The third profile includes those who have never had a religious foundation of any kind. They cannot see themselves participating in any program that uses God, a God of Your Understanding, or a Higher Power. Further, they feel that a program that is centered on religious-oriented activities will not provide a path out of their addiction. Many of the people in this profile, along with the individuals in the second profile, walk away from the most successful addiction recovery program in history.

The 12-Step program is much more than it appears. Although I have no traditional religious foundation and initially responded to the 12-Step program with a high degree of skepticism, I had the great fortune to have good coaching, curiosity, and the desperation of my addiction to compel me to study the program in more detail.

After learning more about the program and practicing it ("working it") successfully, I can tell you that it is a world-class process for addiction recovery. It is built on a solid foundation of medical, psychological, psychiatric, and spiritual influences. It just happens that the 12-Step program is packaged in a religious sounding framework that reflects the influence of the Judeo-Christian organization where the AA founders first observed successful recovery.

If you are someone who has trouble looking past the religious layer of the 12-Step program, some key information regarding the program may change your view and open a door for you. When provided this information, you will be able to read The Big Book and work the 12-Step program without the support of formal religion, a God of Your Understanding, or a Higher Power. If you are someone who has a solid religious foundation, this additional information will enhance your 12-Step program experience.

This book is titled *The Five Keys* because it provides insight into five key areas of the 12-Step program that are not frequently covered in any detail with newcomers to the program. *The Five Keys* will increase your appreciation of the 12-Step program by improving your understanding of the development of the program, its solid technical foundation, and what the program does to help you recover from addiction.

Foundation For The Five Keys

The Newcomer Experience

When you arrive at the point that you begin looking outside of yourself for assistance with your addiction, you are usually not in the best frame of mind. The legal system, family, friends, employers, and/or the desperation of your situation have caused you to seek a solution. You enter this exploration phase with anxiety, apprehension, and a desire for change.

Most of us approach recovery with the hope that it will be a relatively efficient process, something that will get everyone, including the "monkey," off our back in a timely manner. Our addiction of choice has become our principal coping mechanism, a "quick fix," and a way to make ourselves feel comfortable. A solution to our addiction that has some of the same quick-fix characteristics would be convenient.

Although we soon accept that recovery will not be a quick fix, we still hope the process will be straightforward, relatively easy to understand, and that it will provide a clear path to recovery. Unfortunately, for individuals who are looking for a technical rather than a faith-based solution, the 12-Step program is not packaged so that it is straightforward and easy to understand.

Many individuals get their first exposure to the 12 Steps by either reading them on a wall at an addiction rehabilitation center, hearing the 12 Steps read at an AA meeting, or by reading a pamphlet or other handout that lists the 12 Steps. And, as mentioned earlier, some people have the ability to start working the program immediately because their personal beliefs are consistent with the 12 Steps as stated. However, others reject the 12-Step process outright because of its religious tone.

For example, the seventh step reads, "Humbly asked Him to remove our shortcomings." If you are a newcomer without the benefit of any instruction or mentoring, you would interpret this step as having to request a Supreme Being to extract your shortcomings. It is understandable that a person who does not embrace religion as a solution to their addiction might be apprehensive about the program after reading such language. Even people with a strong religious foundation find the seventh step a challenge to interpret and implement.

Another example is the eleventh step, which reads, "Sought through prayer and meditation to improve our conscious contact with God as we understood Him, praying only for knowledge of His will for us and the power to carry that out." A direct interpretation of this, as part of working the program, is that you must pray to an entity, and that His will for you will be revealed to you in a metaphysical way. For those without a solid religious foundation, this is quite a leap of faith.

If you express concern regarding the religious nature of the materials, you are usually provided the following guidance:

- The 12-Step program is not a religious program. It is a spiritual program designed to cause a personal awakening and a change in behavior. It has been successful for many people. You need to have confidence that it will work for you.

- The God mentioned in the 12 Steps is any God of Your Understanding or Higher Power; not the Judeo-Christian God, and

- You should define a God of Your Understanding or Higher Power that you can use to work the program. If you have trouble with this, just use anything outside of yourself to get started. For example, you can use the people at your AA meetings as a "starter" Higher Power, with the understanding that your definition of Higher Power will become more refined as you participate in the program.

For many people, this guidance is insufficient. As you read The Big Book and try to work the 12 Steps, the Judeo-Christian influence is too significant. Even though you have been provided the flexibility to use a God of Your Understanding or a Higher Power, it is still an entity that is similar to the Judeo-Christian God. Further, you have been encouraged to establish a personal relationship with this higher entity to work the program, even if the entity is not "God," per se. Add to this dilemma that you are not typically provided with any detailed information on the 12-Step program's technical history, and you become convinced that this program is not something that will help you overcome your addiction.

Does this sound familiar? One or more of these experiences is common for people having their first exposure to AA and the 12-Step program.

Practical Considerations

In defense of the standard process employed with newcomers to AA, it is important to consider several practical matters related to the global administration of the 12-Step program by AA World Services. Its goal is to have the program be successful, in a standard form, for the largest number of people possible.

First, the core text of The Big Book and its 12 Steps has not been changed since it was originally published in the 1930s. The decision to not change the text and remove the religious layer is strategic on the part of AA World Services. It does not want to tamper with a program that has been successful worldwide for so long.

Second, a "religiously neutral" version of The Big Book published by AA World Services would contradict millions of copies of the current version, available in multiple languages, which exist around the world today. (Note: There have been over 27 million Big Book copies distributed in over 50 languages as of 2010.)

Third, it might be feasible for AA World Services to publish a companion book to The Big Book that would address concerns regarding religion and provide more information on the medical, psychological, and other technical elements that underlie the program. However, this companion book could introduce doubt regarding the original AA materials and the program's general effectiveness. It might also unravel whatever intangible aspects of the program that may be responsible for AA's considerable success.

In general, if AA World Services, treatment centers, and AA groups were to attempt to accommodate everyone's individual religious beliefs, it would make the administration of the 12-Step program incredibly complicated, time-consuming, and confusing to AA newcomers. For people struggling with an addiction and in the early stages of recovery, a drawn-out, multi-faceted introduction to AA would be unproductive.

The generally accepted process of introducing someone to AA is adhered to fairly closely. Facilitators generally introduce the person to the 12 Steps, ask them to use the God of their religion, a God of Your Understanding, or a Higher Power; ask them to begin reading The Big Book; and suggest that they begin working the 12 Steps with a sponsor. There are usually lectures or discussions on religion and other aspects of the program, but a nonreligious interpretation of the materials or a detailed historical profile is not provided.

Early Debate Over Religion

One historical aspect of the AA program that is not widely known is that there was significant debate over religion in the writing and editing of The Big Book in the 1930s. The debate centered on how much, if any, religious-oriented content should be included.

There were several AA members directly involved in writing and editing The Big Book. Within the group doing the work there were Christians, agnostics, and atheists. Some of the members preferred to maintain the Judeo-Christian emphasis, while others wanted it completely removed. The latter group believed the program could stand alone as a technical guide to personal transformation without a religious framework.

Although there are many written accounts of the debate over religion that transpired in the preparation of The Big Book, the most specific evidence is provided by the original manuscript that includes the edits and comments made by the individuals involved in its final review. The original manuscript, including all of the input from the editors, was published by Hazelden in 2010 after being in the possession of several owners for more than 70 years.

As the original manuscript reveals, several areas of The Big Book were softened to reduce the religious emphasis. However, in the end, the founding AA members who wanted to make the material religion neutral did not prevail. The Big Book still leans heavily toward a Judeo-Christian emphasis.

Throughout the years following its publication, AA World Services has been challenged regarding The Big Book's contents, sometimes in articles in prestigious magazines. The organization has been chastised for being ultra conservative in terms of not updating the program's materials to make them more meaningful to a broader audience. Why has AA World Services chosen not to modify The Big Book and its 12 Steps in response to this pressure? The answers lie in the practical considerations highlighted in the previous section of this book.

While several of the founders of AA objected to aspects of The Big Book on religious grounds, many of them were still successful in working the 12-Step program and benefiting from the personal transformation that it provided. Regardless of your view on religion, you can also be successful when armed with the information in *The Five Keys*.

The Five Keys

Background

The five keys include a combination of selected information and tools that will increase your knowledge of the 12-Step program and make the religious layer of the material transparent to you. If you are someone who is working the program with a religious foundation, you will find that the five keys will significantly enhance your recovery experience.

    The five keys accomplish this enhancement by improving your understanding of the program's importance in addiction recovery history, what the program does for you, and by providing some great tools to use in your recovery. The following are brief descriptions of each of the five keys that will be covered in more detail, each with its own section in the book:

1. **An Objective View of AA** – This section provides historical context and significance of The Big Book and its 12-Step program for the treatment of addiction.

2. **Major Program Influences** – In these pages you learn about the people and organizations that influenced the AA founders in the development of the 12-Step program. The list of contributors is impressive and includes medical, psychological, psychiatric, and other professionals.

3. **The Spiritual Transformation** – This section provides an understanding of the most important element of the 12-Step program, the personal, spiritual transformation. This is not a religious conversion or anything of that nature. This transformation is a practical, down-to-earth activity that greatly benefits anyone with an addiction.

4. **Universal Spiritual Principles** – In this section you are provided background on what are

called the "Universal Spiritual Principles." These are guiding principles that become an external source of inspiration, something outside of you to use for your addiction recovery. Call these a Higher Power for your 12-Step program if you like, but having these as a reference point for your program will completely eliminate the need to have a God of Your Understanding or a Higher Power of the Judeo-Christian type. Your guidance will come directly from the universal principles.

5. **Neutral 12 Steps** – This section provides a version of each of the 12 Steps that does not include any references to Higher Power, God of Your Understanding, prayer, or any related element. This version of the 12 Steps conveys the underlying intent and purpose of each step, but without the religious content.

An Objective View of AA
Key #1

The Big Book and the 12-Step program outlined in its pages are historically significant and groundbreaking for the treatment of alcoholism. Unfortunately, the historical context and significance of the AA program is not addressed in much detail in The Big Book. The majority of AA program participants are not exposed to the detailed historical aspects of AA, if at all, until later in their recovery. If they gain this additional insight, it is normally from books, articles, and documentation of speeches by AA members and historians.

Having an understanding of the historical significance of the AA program is useful, but it is particularly important to those who struggle with the religious nature of the material and the prospect that there is nothing much underlying it. Along with an understanding of the major influences on the development of the program (Key #2), a person can read The Big Book and work the 12-Step program with a more objective viewpoint. The subject matter of this section is a snapshot of the history of alcoholism treatment in the United States and the role of the 12-Step program in this history.

The history of the United States is rich in failed attempts to address alcoholism. The social movements and recovery techniques attempted from 1700 to 1930 exhibit similar patterns of becoming popular quickly and then rapidly declining in popularity and effectiveness. The reasons for their demise are numerous, but the central theme is that the programs usually helped a person to stop drinking, but they failed to provide a path for sustaining sobriety.

It is worth noting that many of these failed attempts included elements that were highly effective. Several of these elements would eventually be incorporated into The Big Book and its 12-Step program such as complete abstinence from drinking, detoxification (detox), anonymity, and mutual support groups.

Examples of attempts to address alcohol addiction in the pre-AA period, from 1700-1930, include the following (dates noted when appropriate):

- Benjamin Rush, M.D. – Popularized the concept that alcoholism was a disease and treated it by inducing vomiting, frightening the patient, drawing large amounts of blood, and other methods (1784).

- Temperance Movement – Focused on activities designed to raise public awareness about the benefits of drinking in moderation, but eventually altered the message to advocate abstinence as the only viable solution to what was perceived as a widespread social disease (1800).

- Washingtonian Movement – Added to the rehabilitation picture the goal of reforming alcoholics by encouraging them to publicly share their alcoholism-related experiences as well as their recovery process. The movement's adherents believed that temperance was not enough (1840).

- Fraternal Temperance Societies / Reform Clubs – Mutual-aid groups established to help each other, bringing the concept of anonymity to the scene of addiction treatment. Some groups even had secret passwords and handshakes (1840).

- <u>Inebriate Facilities</u> – Large, medically run facilities that were operated by alcoholism specialists. They offered detox, residential services, day treatment, and outpatient care services, versions of which are widely used today (1870).

- <u>Miracle Cures</u> – Potions and elixirs to cure alcoholism. Many contained a high percentage of alcohol (Hostettler's Stomach Bitters had 44% alcohol content!) (1880).

- <u>Religious Conversion</u> – Missions and other organizations oriented to help alcoholics improve their moral lifestyle through religious affiliation and beliefs (various dates).

- <u>Physical Treatment</u> – Included electroshock therapy, surgical lobotomies, sterilization, drugs, diets, exercise, work, and many other approaches (various dates).

- <u>Psychological Care</u> – Approached alcoholism from the standpoint that a personal psychosis or disordered personality was the cause, and that unmanageable alcohol consumption was a symptom of the illness (various dates).

- <u>Prohibition</u> – National law implemented to make the production and sale of alcohol illegal in the United States (1920-1933).

Like many great discoveries, there were people experimenting in the general vicinity of what would eventually become the AA recovery solution. And, as with many great discoveries, there was someone with the insight, intuition, intellectual capacity, and correct timing to put all of the pieces of the puzzle together into a cohesive picture. As it relates to recovery from alcohol addiction in 1930's America, those people were Bill Wilson and Dr. Bob Smith. They are widely recognized as the principal founders of Alcoholics Anonymous.

The AA program was a revolution in addiction treatment because it introduced a combination of abstinence, personal transformation, and a process for maintaining a sober condition over time. It represented an integration of the effective aspects of past attempts at treating addiction with innovations made by the founding members of AA.

The concepts and working principles assembled in The Big Book and 12-Step program by Bill Wilson and his associates were a significant undertaking. If you consider the content of The Big Book closely, it is a world-class synthesis of medical, psychological, psychiatric, and spiritual principles. Many view the development of The Big Book as an incredible feat, especially considering that the authors and editors were alcoholics in relatively early stages of recovery.

What made this accomplishment feasible, in part, was that the group of recovering alcoholics who were involved in the preparation of The Big Book included many intelligent and talented individuals. This group had first-hand experience with the disease of alcoholism, success with the program they were active in, and the motivation to share this with others.

Major Program Influences
Key #2

An initial look at The Big Book and its 12 Steps might leave one with the impression that it is largely a philosophical program without much technical merit. It is considerably more than that.

The AA program was developed with the insight of medical, psychological, psychiatric, and spiritual professionals, and with field testing by recovering alcoholics. Although there were many influences on the development of the AA program, there are several that stand out.

William D. Silkworth, M.D.

Silkworth, who was one of Bill Wilson's physicians during his inpatient treatment, was a neurologist and specialist in alcoholism. It was Dr. Silkworth who provided Bill the input that alcoholism is an "allergy of the body," coupled with an "obsession of the mind." Silkworth believed that alcoholism is a progressive disease and, when left untreated, would likely result in death. He advanced that the alcoholic must commit to abstinence, go through a detox process, and "experience a transformation from a moral psychology standpoint." In other words, an alcoholic must transform his fundamental character.

Silkworth was assertive in promoting his views on the physical illness, mental obsession, and the moral rehabilitation aspects of alcoholism. He staked his reputation by aggressively supporting Bill Wilson in his work with alcoholics.

William James

James was a Harvard professor of psychology and philosophy. He is considered by some to be the father of modern psychology.

Ebby Thacher, a recovering alcoholic (more on Thacher later), gave Bill Wilson a copy of James' book, *The Varieties of Religious Experiences*. Thacher gave the book to Wilson while he was being treated for alcoholism in Towns Hospital in New York City. The book, a documentation of lectures delivered by James in 1901 and 1902, is still used today as a reference in the fields of psychology, religion, and philosophy.

James' book provided many concepts that Wilson would use to develop the 12-Step program. Three of these are worth noting here. First, a person is positioned for a complete personal transformation when they reach a point of hopelessness (they are "powerless"). James maintained that a person at the point of desperation and deflation has a mental environment for a real change in fundamental thinking and behavior. Second, the nature of that change is "letting go" of one's ego and self-centered thinking ("turning your will over"). The individual must then embrace a set of higher spiritual principles that has the welfare of others at its center. Third, the spiritual principles can come from whatever a person considers the "divine"; something outside of themselves ("the higher power"). Organized religion might be one of these sources, but not the only one. For the purpose of this book, *The Five Keys*, a list of universal spiritual principles will be that source of inspiration.

Carl Jung, M.D.

Jung was a Swiss psychotherapist and psychiatrist who founded the field of analytical psychology. He is responsible for many notable advances in the field of psychology, including the concept of personality archetypes, which are the foundation of several modern personality testing tools. He is also one of the fathers of modern dream analysis.

In 1931, a young, wealthy individual, Rowland Hazard, was undergoing psychoanalysis in Switzerland with Jung. Rowland had tried all methods known to someone of his wealth and access to address his addiction to alcohol. He spent nearly a year under Jung's care but relapsed when he returned to the United States. In a disillusioned state he returned to Jung, who informed Hazard that curing his condition was probably beyond the capabilities of conventional medicine and psychiatry, and that it would take a spiritual transformation to overcome a malady of this nature.

Jung's work reinforced William James' observations regarding the spiritual transformation but with a medical and psychiatric emphasis. Rowland heeded Jung's advice and returned to the United States to seek a spiritual transformation, which led him to the Oxford Group.

<u>The Oxford Group</u>

The Oxford Group was a non-denominational, Christian fellowship founded by Franklin Buchman. Buchman, a Lutheran minister who had experience with personal "conversions" (transformations), started the Oxford Group in 1921.

The process for facilitating a spiritual transformation in a person was the major contribution of the Oxford Group to AA's 12-Step program. The Oxford Group's focus was to convert "sinners" which, of course, included alcoholics. They introduced into the 12-Step program the concepts of self-survey, confessing one's defects, and having the willingness to make restitution.

Ebby Thacher, the friend of Bill Wilson mentioned earlier, introduced Bill to the Oxford Group. Thacher, once a hopeless alcoholic, had gone through a complete personal transformation using the Oxford Group's principles. Witnessing Thacher's transformation created Wilson's interest in the Oxford Group and eventually led to his participation in the group's meetings. As it happened, the Oxford Group was a Christian-based organization. The Big Book and its 12 Steps ended up being written in the language of that group, with a Judeo-Christian emphasis.

If Bill had made the same discovery at a Buddhist temple or some experimental psychology clinic, the language of The Big Book and its 12 Steps might have been different.

Practical Experience With Alcoholics

Beginning with the visit from Ebby Thacher, Bill Wilson began to see the benefits of working with other recovering alcoholics. Willingness to listen to, take direction from, and share honestly with another person who understands your situation seems practical and obvious. However, it turned out to be especially profound in the context of addiction recovery. Bill Wilson, Bob Smith, and others saw the positive impact of mutual support many times in their work with alcoholics. Examples of working with others in the AA context include group meetings, one-on-one sponsorships, and open talks.

Wilson used the Oxford Group meetings as the focal point for alcoholism recovery in the early stages of developing AA, but he eventually broke away from the Oxford Group. Wilson found that certain aspects of the Oxford Group sessions were not effective for alcoholism recovery. Specifically, the Oxford Group members' names were not kept anonymous, their practices were too "absolute," and the group operated on the basis of promotion rather than attraction.

The Spiritual Transformation
Key #3

At the center of the addiction recovery revolution brought on by AA is the discovery that the alcoholic must undergo a spiritual transformation as the path out of addiction. The primary purpose of the 12-Step program, the discussions at the AA meetings, and the one-on-one work with a sponsor is to facilitate that transformation. The 12-Step work also provides a method of maintaining an improved lifestyle over the long term.

What is vital to understand is that a spiritual transformation is not a religious conversion, a born-again religious experience, or anything of that nature. A person with a religious foundation prior to participating in AA can find support for the 12-Step program in religion, but nonreligious sources of inspiration and guidance are equally effective. Later in this book, you will be provided a list of Universal Spiritual Principles that can be used in conjunction with your 12-Step work and spiritual transformation.

Whether you call it a change in your moral fabric, a personal transition, or assign it any other label, a spiritual transformation is imperative in that it represents a transition in how you view yourself, how you view life, your goals, and what you focus on as realistic concerns. This spiritual transformation is required because it is an unhealthy view of yourself and dysfunctional interactions with others which are the underlying reasons for your addiction. This "stinking thinking," as it is referred to in the AA community, results in low self-esteem and self-centered behavior.

The genesis of an individual's stinking thinking can come from traumatic life experiences or even from what some people might consider fairly routine personal experiences. As examples, some individuals experience years of living in an abusive family environment that gives them a distorted view of the world and a poor view of themselves. Taking it to the other extreme, as a teenager, a person might have suffered negative experiences with a member of the opposite sex or have been chastised by friends about their physical characteristics. Both of these scenarios can send someone on the path of self-deprecation and low self-esteem.

As a reprieve from the anxiety associated with dysfunctional thinking, and often unconsciously, a person turns to alcohol, drugs, gambling, or another distraction. Once the physical addiction sets in, there is no amount of willpower that will overcome it. A spiritual transformation is the only long-term solution to emerging from this predicament. By working through the 12 Steps, discussing issues at AA meetings, interacting with a sponsor, and participating in other related AA activities, a person gradually experiences the required spiritual transformation. There are no guarantees, but as they say around the AA community, "It works if you work it!"

There are several phases that you will experience in your spiritual transformation. Each one corresponds to one or more of the 12 Steps.

Phase 1 - Acceptance

In the first phase, you begin by honestly acknowledging the desperate state of your affairs. Then, as a starting point for your spiritual transformation, you abstain from using alcohol, drugs, or participating in any other addictive activity. A clear head is a prerequisite to successful, long-term recovery.

In this first phase, you also accept that the disease is progressive and that it is not simply a matter of "turning your willpower into high gear" to solve the problem. Once your addiction integrates itself into your body chemistry and brain function, you are powerless over it and cannot stop it by simply trying harder. (Step one of the 12 Steps is generally where these subjects are explored.)

Phase 2 - Surrender

In the second phase, you surrender to the fact that any recovery plan designed by an addict (you) is destined for failure. Your physical dependence and mental obsession make it impossible for you to be objective.

As part of this phase, you learn that to successfully recover from addiction, you must turn yourself over 100 percent to powers outside of yourself for guidance. For many people these powers include the medical community, addiction recovery professionals, members of the AA fellowship, spiritual advisors, and/or a personal God. (In the 12-Step program, these subjects are normally addressed in steps two and three.)

Phase 3 - Exploration

In this phase, you will develop an understanding of yourself and the thinking process that is at the source of your addiction. This is accomplished in two parts. First, you document (list) your fears, resentments, and other concerns, as well as your role in each. Second, you have one or more discussions with a trusted person regarding the items you have identified in your personal inventory. Both of these activities are enlightening and rewarding and set you on the path to transformation.

The result of phase three is that you will develop an understanding of the changes in your character traits, and the underlying spiritual principles, that will improve your interactions with yourself and others. This phase also makes a significant contribution to your willingness to be open and honest with yourself and others. (Steps four and five of the 12-Step program address personal exploration.)

Phase 4 - Transition

In this phase, you first begin putting your character changes to work for you, which involves resolving to conduct your thinking in a manner that is consistent with the information that you learned about yourself in the Exploration phase. Next, you take the new you into the world. On a day-to-day basis you demonstrate your new character traits which markedly contrast with your self-centered behavior of the past. (Steps six and seven of the 12-Step program are when this transition is experienced.)

Phase 5 - Reconnection

In this phase of the spiritual transformation, you make amends to individuals that you have adversely affected with your addiction and develop tools to maintain solid relationships with these people going forward.

The first part of this phase involves making a list of all the people you have wronged. You discuss with these people the work you are doing to remain sober, make good on any past indiscretions, and reconnect with them on a personal level. As a result of these actions you learn that you are making amends as much for yourself as for the other person. It is important for you to eliminate the baggage of the past.

The second part of this phase is to make an effort every day, in everything that you do, to recognize when you are slipping into old behaviors and to make immediate amends when you do so. (Steps eight, nine, and ten are when these aspects of your transformation are undertaken.)

Phase 6 - Maintenance

This phase involves staying connected to the principles of the 12-Step program by keeping in mind your new character traits; ensuring that they are always fresh in the forefront of your thinking. This ongoing awareness can be accomplished using meditation, calm reflection, and other techniques. The underlying goal is to always use the program and spiritual principles to guide you in your decision making and actions. (This is step eleven of the 12 Steps.)

Phase 7 - Collaboration

In this final phase, you make a commitment to two important activities that help with your well-being and the well-being of others who are suffering from addiction. First, you make the commitment and take action to share your experience, strength, and hope with others who are seeking their way out of addiction. This can come in a number of forms, such as continued attendance and sharing at your group AA meetings, one-on-one sponsorships, and participating in open talks. Second, you begin the lifelong process of practicing the principles of the program and your new and improved character in all of your daily activities. (This phase is represented by step twelve of the 12-Step program.)

Individuals who actively work through all of these phases using the 12-Step program will experience a gradual spiritual transformation and a corresponding elimination of the obsession regarding their addiction. This transformation works where the cold turkey, white-knuckle attempts of the past failed. It works because the spiritual transformation addresses the cause of the addiction rather than treating the symptoms.

Universal Spiritual Principles
Key #4

All of the major nonreligious and religious belief systems in the world have the same guiding principles at their core. These principles, which we will call the Universal Spiritual Principles, represent healthy practices for living that promote solid relationships with human beings, other living creatures, the physical environment, and with ourselves. Individuals who live by these spiritual principles are generally referred to as "people who have great character."

People who have issues with addiction are generally not conducting their lives in a solid, spiritual manner. They act in a self-centered manner and have self-esteem issues as a result of a poor relationship with themselves and others. Alcohol, drugs, and/or addictive behaviors are used as compensation.

The 12-Step program effects a transformation to an improved lifestyle that is consistent with the Universal Spiritual Principles. Whether you have deep religious beliefs or are a dedicated atheist, these principles are essential to your spiritual transformation. People generally find these principles easy to embrace because they make sense. However, having a relationship with a God or deity as an intermediary to the Universal Spiritual Principles causes a problem for some. Having to take direction, seek advice from, and pray to a physical or metaphysical embodiment of a human being will simply not work.

If you are one of these people, the most effective method for using the Universal Spiritual Principles is to remove the higher entity from the picture altogether and make your relationship directly with the list of principles. Call these principles your Higher Power if you like, but the primary goal is to allow these principles to guide all of your thinking and actions.

Universal Spiritual Principles

- The Golden Rule / Law of Reciprocity – Treat others as you want them to treat you. This is the cornerstone of all major nonreligious and religious belief systems in the world.

- Honesty – Be truthful, sincere, and candid with yourself and others.

- Humility – Have a modest opinion of yourself relative to others, and behave accordingly.

- <u>Non-Judgmental</u> – Do not evaluate and condemn others, which is self-promoting and delusional behavior.

- <u>Forgiving</u> – Cease to feel resentment toward others. Be empathetic and pardoning.

- <u>Generosity</u> – Act in a liberal, giving, and sharing manner toward others.

- <u>Compassion</u> – Have deep sympathy for others' misfortunes and a strong desire to alleviate their suffering.

- <u>Happiness Is Within</u> – Do not seek happiness in things, people, or events. Seek it through having an understanding and acceptance of yourself.

- <u>We Create Our Own Destiny</u> – You have free will. Your choices determine what befalls you.

- <u>Responsibility / Commitment</u> – Have the capacity to adhere to your commitments and follow through on promises.

- <u>Moderation</u> – Exercise restraint, avoid extremes, and practice temperance.

- <u>Know And Respect Yourself</u> – Appreciate yourself for who you are without focusing on who you are not.

- <u>Deep Respect For All Life</u> – Do not kill, harm, or abuse people, animals, or the planet's resources.

- <u>Don't Steal</u> – Have respect for the possessions of others. Come by your possessions through productive work and contributions of your own.

- <u>Speak Gently</u> – Do not be false, slanderous, harsh, or prone to idle chatter.

- <u>All Things Change</u> – Live your life expecting things and circumstances to change. Do not cling to a particular state of being or definition of yourself.

You should use these principles as the guide for your thoughts and actions. Operating with these principles will shift your focus from a self-centered way of living to a more balanced, serene existence with others and your environment.

Neutral 12 Steps
Key #5

In this section, you are provided a version of each of the 12 Steps that have references to Higher Power, God of Your Understanding, prayer, and related elements removed. Some background information on the evolution of the 12 Steps is beneficial before reviewing these modified 12 Steps.

The 12 Steps were influenced by the guiding principles of the Oxford Group, which included what they called the "Five C's" for transforming "sinners," including addicts.

The Five C's

- Confidence
- Confession
- Conviction
- Conversion
- Continuance

These Five C's were supported by four morality standards called the "Four Absolutes":

The Four Absolutes

- Honesty
- Purity
- Unselfishness
- Love

When Bill Wilson and his associates formed a fellowship that was separate from the Oxford Group, they began using a word-of-mouth program made up of six informal steps:

The "Word-of-Mouth" Program

1. We admitted that we were powerless over alcohol.

2. We got honest with ourselves.

3. We got honest with another person, in confidence.

4. We made amends for harms done others.

5. We worked with other alcoholics without demand for prestige or money.

6. We prayed to God to help us do these things as best we could.

The six "word of mouth" steps were formalized and expanded by Wilson into the 12-Step program. Interestingly, and despite Wilson coming from an agnostic background, the 12 Steps took on an even more religious tone. Perhaps he was concerned about losing whatever intangible aspects that were working for the Oxford Group.

12 Steps (From The Big Book of AA)

1. We admitted we were powerless over alcohol – that our lives had become unmanageable.

2. Came to believe that a Power greater than ourselves could restore us to sanity.

3. Made a decision to turn our will and our lives over to the care of God *as we understood Him*.

4. Made a searching and fearless moral inventory of ourselves.

5. Admitted to God, to ourselves, and to another human being the exact nature of our wrongs.

6. Were entirely ready to have God remove all these defects of character.

7. Humbly asked Him to remove our shortcomings.

8. Made a list of all persons we had harmed, and became willing to make amends to them all.

9. Made direct amends to such people wherever possible, except when to do so would injure them or others.

10. Continued to take personal inventory and when we were wrong promptly admitted it.

11. Sought through prayer and meditation to improve our conscious contact with God *as we understood Him*, praying only for knowledge of His will for us and the power to carry that out.

12. Having had a spiritual awakening as the result of these steps, we tried to carry this message to alcoholics, and to practice these principles in all our affairs.

The following version of the 12 Steps has the religious content removed and some additional information added for clarity. In this version, the term "spiritual" refers specifically to the Universal Spiritual Principles that were introduced in the previous section of this book.

Neutral 12 Steps

1. We admitted that we were powerless over our addiction, that it is a progressive disease, and that it is having a devastating impact on our lives.

2. Came to believe that medical, psychological, and spiritual resources outside of us must be used to overcome our addiction and return us to a better state of living.

3. Made a decision to take 100 percent of our direction from spiritual and other recovery resources outside of ourselves, and that we

would abandon using personal willpower and our own plans to address our addiction.

4. Made an honest and thorough inventory of our resentments, fears, sexual misgivings, and related issues, with a specific focus on understanding our role in each of these.

5. Admitted to ourselves and to another person the exact nature of our wrongs and the defects of character behind the misconduct.

6. Were entirely ready to change ourselves by addressing the character issues that we identified in steps four and five.

7. Humbly, honestly, and on a day-to-day basis, we will use the spiritual principles as a guide for our behavior.

8. Made a list of all persons we affected with our addiction, and became willing to make amends for our indiscretions and to let these people know about the changes we are making.

9. Made direct amends to the people on our list, except when to do so would injure them or others.

10. Continued to take personal inventory with respect to our daily actions, and when we were exhibiting old behaviors we promptly made amends to the individuals involved.

11. Sought through meditation, study, and reflection to improve our awareness of the principles of the AA program, the spiritual principles, and our ability to carry these out on a daily basis.

12. Having realized the benefits of the 12-Step program, we try to bring this information to other addicts and to practice the principles of the program in all of our affairs.

When you are using the 12 Steps at meetings, working with your sponsor, and in other activities, you should reflect on these "Neutral 12 Steps." Combined with the Universal Spiritual Principles, this modified version of the 12 Steps will position you for a successful recovery experience.

Making It Work For You

Armed with the information provided in this book, you can begin the process of working the 12-Step program in a manner that fits with your personal beliefs. A few suggestions will help you move forward in a productive way.

Terminology

If you are not someone with a strong religious foundation, you will need a technique for dealing with language and terminology used in various activities in the program. These include prayer, turning your will over to God, and similar tasks.

The issue of terminology is actually easy to overcome as long as you keep in mind that your primary source of inspiration and guidance is the Universal Spiritual Principles. Further, you now have an alternative version of the 12 Steps, in a religion neutral form, upon which you can always reflect.

Essentially, all of the requirements of the program that have a religious-oriented action associated with them suggest interaction with a God or Higher Power, and virtually all of these actions are a request for inspiration or guidance of a spiritual nature. These actions will be familiar to you if you approach the program with the formal support of your religion; however, if you are working the program without a God, it is straightforward to think of yourself as having all of your "interactions" directly with the Universal Spiritual Principles.

For example, praying to God for guidance means looking to the list of Universal Spiritual Principles for inspiration in your area of concern. Turning your will over to God would mean letting the list of Universal Spiritual Principles drive your thinking and actions. Maintaining a conscious contact with God translates to having a solid understanding and awareness of the Universal Spiritual Principles at all times.

A complete list of all possible interactions of this type is not possible to cover in this book, but employing the simple rule of making your "interactions" directly with the list of Universal Spiritual Principles should handle all of the situations you encounter.

<u>Articulating Your Position</u>

An area where some suggestions are in order relates to situations where you may feel that it is appropriate to let people know your position regarding God or a Higher Power. For example, when you are involved in group or one-on-one discussions the subject of God and Higher Power could surface in the context of how you get your inspiration.

If you are working the program with support of a God or Higher Power, let them know that. Otherwise, let them know that your Higher Power is a set of Universal Spiritual Principles from which you derive your guidance and direction. If you believe that further clarification is necessary, let them know that these spiritual principles are common to all of the major philosophies and religions of the world, but that you do not have a personal God or Higher Power as part of your relationship with these principles.

Being Self-Promoting

It is important that you are not an evangelist and that you are not aggressive with others regarding your beliefs. In this area, you should exercise caution. As you are aware, addiction recovery is difficult for everyone involved, and it is important that each person be allowed to work the program within their own belief system and comfort zone.

Part of being a good AA citizen, from a spiritual standpoint, is not to impose your own beliefs on others. The best way to be this good citizen is to make your comments and questions as religion neutral as possible when sharing at a 12-Step meeting or any other forum. If you encounter individuals who are struggling with the religious content of the AA materials, take them aside, share what you have learned, and let them know about the alternatives available.

Facilities

One fact that becomes obvious to people participating in the program is that a large number of meetings are held in churches and other religious facilities. To newcomers who are uncomfortable with formal religion, they may feel as if they are attending some form of a Bible meeting. This is not the case.

Churches certainly provide a pleasant environment for those people with strong religious beliefs, but the primary reason meetings are held in churches is that the facilities represent an inexpensive and relatively anonymous place to have an AA meeting. Further, church administrators are usually eager to be of service to their community.

AA Meetings - Composition

The value of AA meetings cannot be overemphasized because the group discussions regarding personal development that take place at these meetings are invaluable. However, it is important that you experiment with different meetings to find those that you are most comfortable attending.

You will find entire meetings that have a strong religious emphasis, others that are relatively neutral, and others that might lean in an agnostic direction. If you are uncomfortable with a particular meeting, seek an alternative. In the end, you will find that most of the AA meetings have a good mix of people who are respectful of the personal beliefs of others in attendance.

AA Meetings - Opening and Closing

Each AA meeting opens in a slightly different manner, which is determined by several factors. What is fairly consistent at meetings is that some combination of the AA Preamble, Promises, and How It Works is used. At the close of the meeting, it is typical to use either the Serenity Prayer or The Lord's Prayer.

The Promises and How It Works contain content that may not fit with your personal beliefs. You should look to the tools that you have been provided in *The Five Keys* for your guidance in this area. With respect to closing prayers, you have the option of remaining quiet. However, many people, regardless of their beliefs, participate in the closing to show unity with the group and the program.

The 12 Steps

The single item you will be most exposed to in the AA program is the list of the 12 Steps. These are often read at the opening of AA meetings, frequently the subject of sharing at AA meeting tables, and central to discussions with a sponsor. There is one simple suggestion for those of you who are working the program without a God. Keep the Neutral 12 Steps in mind. They will serve you well wherever you go.

Bibliography

- Ernest Kurtz - *Not God* - Hazelden - 1991

- Anonymous - *The Book That Started It All* - Hazelden - 2010

- William L. White - *Slaying The Dragon* - Chestnut Health Systems - 1998

- Dale Mitchel - *Silkworth: The Little Doctor Who Loved Drunks* - Hazelden - 2002

- Various - *Alcoholics Anonymous* - AA World Services - 2008

- Mitchell K. - "The Big Book Goes To Press" - The Silkworth Mitchell K. Library - Date Unknown

- Michelle Boorstein - "AA Original Manuscript Reveals Profound Debate Over Religion" - Washington Post - 2010

- Griffith Edwards - *Alcohol: The World's Favorite Drug* - Thomas Dunne Books - 2002

- Susan Cheever - "Time 100: Bill Wilson"- Time Magazine - 1999

- Fr. Robert J. Roth - "William James and Alcoholics Anonymous" - America - 1965

Bibliography
(Continued)

- William D. Silkworth - "Alcoholism as a Manifestation of Allergy" - Central Park West Medical Record - 1937

- William James - *The Varieties of Religious Experiences: A Study In Human Nature* - Longsmans, Green & Company - 1902

- Jerome Levin - *Introduction to Alcoholism Counseling* - Taylor & Francis - 1990

- Alcoholics Anonymous World Services - *Pass It On: The Story of Bill Wilson and How the AA Message Reached the World* - AA World Services - 1984

- Bill Wilson - "Where Did the 12 Steps Come From?" - AA Grapevine - 1953

- Linda Mercadante - *Victims and Sinners* - Westminster John Knox Press - 1996

- Raymond F. Paloutzian, PhD and Crystal L. Park, PhD - *Handbook of the Psychology of Religion and Spirituality* - The Guilford Press - 2005

- Jeffery Moses - *Oneness* -The Ballantine Publishing Group - 2002

About The Author

Archer Voxx is an accomplished writer and a recovering alcoholic and addict. He has used the 12-Step program of Alcoholics Anonymous successfully for his recovery.

The Five Keys is based on experience gained through inpatient and outpatient treatment, addiction therapy, the 12-Step program, and research for this book. In addition to his work in the AA community, he is a resource for family groups and Al-Anon participants who are seeking help for friends and family who suffer from addiction.

Appendix

Character Traits

The list of character traits provided in the next few pages is an outstanding tool for the personal transformation work in steps four through seven of the 12-Step program. As a warm-up exercise to this work, review the list of character liabilities and assets. Understanding yourself in the context of the list is very valuable.

Liability	**Asset**
Aggressive	Gentle
Angry	Content
Apathetic	Interested
Apprehensive	Courageous
Argumentative	Agreeable
Arrogant	Humble
Attacking	Self-restrained
Avoidant	Responsible
Boastful	Modest
Careless	Painstaking
Cheating	Honest

Liability	**Asset**
Competitive (socially)	Cooperative
Conceited	Humble
Contradictory	Agreeable
Contrary	Compromising
Controlling	Sharing
Cowardly	Brave
Critical	Non-judgmental
Cynical	Optimistic
Deceitful	Honest
Defensive	Open-minded
Defiant	Respectful
Denying	Accepting
Dependent	Self-reliant
Depressed	Hopeful
Dirty	Clean
Dishonest	Honest
Disloyal	Faithful
Disobedient	Responsible
Disrespectful	Reverent
Enabling	Supportive
Envying	Confident

Liability	**Asset**
Evasive	Direct
Exaggerating	Modest
Falsely modest	Honest
False pride	Humility
Fantasizing	Realistic
Fearful	Confident
Forgetful	Responsible
Gluttonous	Moderate
Gossiping	Praising
Greedy	Generous
Hateful	Forgiving
Hypersensitive	Tolerant
Ill-tempered	Good-natured
Impatient	Tolerant
Impulsive	Disciplined
Inconsiderate	Thoughtful
Indecisive	Resolute
Indifferent	Caring
Inflexible	Open-minded
Insecure	Self-confident

Liability	**Asset**
Intolerant	Patient
Irresponsible	Reliable
Isolating	Outgoing
Jealous	Trusting
Judgmental	Tolerant
Justifying	Candid
Lacking purpose	Earnest
Lazy	Industrious
Loud	Soft-spoken
Lustful	Respectful
Lying	Honest
Manipulative	Non-controlling
Masked	Open
Nagging	Supportive
Narrow minded	Flexible
Obscene	Decent
Over emotional	Level-headed
Perfectionist	Realistic
Pessimistic	Optimistic
Possessive	Generous
Prejudiced	Open-minded

Liability	**Asset**
Procrastinating	Action-oriented
Rationalizing	Accepting
Resentful	Content
Resisting change	Open-minded
Rude	Courteous
Sarcastic	Kind
Self-important	Humble
Self-centered	Caring
Self-hating	Self-accepting
Self-pitying	Grateful
Self-righteous	Humble
Self-seeking	Concerned for others
Shy	Outgoing
Spiteful	Loving
Stealing	Giving
Stubborn	Willing
Sullen	Cheerful
Superior	Humble
Superstitious	Realistic
Suspicious	Trusting
Tense	Serene

Liability	**Asset**
Thinking negatively	Thinking positively
Treacherous	Honest
Undisciplined	Organized
Unfair	Just
Unfriendly	Cordial
Ungrateful	Thankful
Unkind	Benevolent
Unsupportive	Encouraging
Untrustworthy	Reliable
Useless	Helpful
Vain	Modest
Vindictive	Forgiving
Violent	Gentle
Vulgar	Polite
Wasteful	Thrifty
Willful	Yielding
Withdrawn	Outgoing
Verbose	Succinct

Personal Notes

Printed in Dunstable, United Kingdom